D1561373

TWISTED YEARS

YEARS

A Memoir of an American Soldier in WWI

John B. Smith

These are the writings of John B. Smith aka Jack Smith. No attempt was made to make corrections in spelling or punctuation. Artificial breaks were added to make reading more pleasureable.

No part of this publication may be reproduced or transmitted in any form without approval.

Library of Congress Control Number: 2015935965
Copyright 2015 by Ellen Bogner

Cover and interior design by Christine Keleny of CKBooks Publishing - ckbookspublishing.com

✠

Dedicated to the memory of my buddies
who were killed in action during the World War;
to those who are sick in institutions;
to those who are destitute and alone;
to those who lie in unknown graves:
and to those old comrades of 1916 - 1917 - 1918
where ever they are.

FORWARD

A time to love and a time to hate, A time of war and a time of peace. Ecclesiastes 3:8

The three-ring notebook, musty smelling and battered by the time I pulled it out, was in a box in my attic. In the mid-1930s my maternal grandfather, John Bernhardt Smith, wrote his memoir of his years with the 127th Infantry, E company, 32nd Division of the Wisconsin National Guard. His hope was to someday publish his memoir, his book as he called it, but it never happened.

As kids we knew about Grandpa's book, that it was his story of WWI and that he also had a collection of letters and flags from the countries involved in the War. I was only allowed to read a censored version as it was considered too graphic for a girl to read. Consequently I first read it in its entirety a few years ago. I was moved by his story, but I returned the notebook to storage in the attic.

In February 2015 I was reading a novel about medical workers in WWI and I remembered my Grandpa's story of WWI. I went up to the attic and dug around in some boxes and found the notebook. I read the story twice and then gave it to my husband to read. I realized it was a story that needed to be shared and also to fulfill Grandpa's lost dream of publishing his book.

The story starts in 1916, almost a century ago. There are no living WWI veterans, those millions of soldiers have had their stories silenced by time, similar to that eleventh day in November 1918 when the guns of the Great War were silenced.

John B. Smith was a humble man. He had been awarded the Purple Heart medal for being wounded and the Oak Leaf Cluster for being gassed in service to his country. These honors are never mentioned in his memoir.

John Bernhardt Smith, also known as JB or Jack and as a child Johnny, was born in Eau Claire, Wisconsin on September 20, 1897. His mother, Karen Johanesen, emigrated from Norway and his father, John Bernhardt Sr, from Sweden. JB had two brothers and five sisters. His mother died in 1904 and he was raised by his older sisters. His father worked as a carpenter to support the family. After the war JB married Margaret Lemke on September 8, 1920 in Eau Claire. They moved to Milwaukee, Wisconsin where he worked for the Internal Revenue Service as head of the accounting division. JB served in the Army Reserves from 1920 to 1940 and retired with the rank of Captain. He retired from the IRS in 1957 and they moved to Fort Atkinson, Wisconsin to be near their only child, Elaine, and her husband, Kenneth Pattow, and their three daughters.

JB had an active retirement until his death in 1977. He was Commander of the local WWI Veterans group and active in his church and the Masonic organization.

He was chaplain of the local American Legion and in that capacity gave the Memorial Day address in Lake Mills, Wisconsin in 1970, which is included in this book. He was also the last Justice of the Peace in Fort Atkinson.

JB was a loving grandfather who taught his three granddaughters the importance of service to others and love of country, by his example. I am the oldest granddaughter and this book honors John B. Smith and the millions of soldiers and medical workers who served, fought and died in WWI.

This book is also dedicated to Samuel, born in 2014, John B. Smith's great-great-grandson, in the hope that he will always know peace and not war.

Ellen Bogner
March 2015

TWISTED
YEARS

In this brief accounting of three twisted years, I have set forth only the outstanding events and dates. No effort has been made to use perfectly correct English, but the story is simply told as from a common soldier to a friend. Many of the dates are not correct, as time has erased from my memory many of the exact dates, but they are within a very few days of being correct. The many incidents described, however, are told just as they occurred, and, if you can read between the lines, you will discover humor, sadness, patriotism, desertion from principle, love, hate and kindness all interwoven into the lives of young men - boys - many of whom died, many of whom are now fine examples of American manhood, many of whom are now ordinary bums, all the result of those three twisted years.

✠

During the Spring of 1916, when bands of Mexican outlaws under the leadership of Pancho Villa, were making raids into the state of New Mexico. Particularly in the vicinity of Columbus, a rising feeling of resentment was growing in the United States against those irregulars over whom the Mexican government apparently had no control. The climax was reached when several Americans were killed on United States soil, and this government decided to organize a punitive expeditionary force and either destroy or disperse the outlaws.

An expeditionary force, consisting entirely of regulars, was organized with the approval of the Mexican government. It was commanded by General John J. Pershing, under the direction of General Fritz Funston, with headquarters at San Antonio, Texas. Immediately following the organization of the expeditionary force, the National Guard was called to the colors and given orders to recruit up to full war strength.

TEXAS

The afternoon of June 20th, 1916, I was shingling the roof of the new parsonage of the Second Congregational Church (which my father was building) on Bellinger Street, in Eau Claire, Wisconsin. Presently I heard a band playing a military march down town to bolster up business for Company "E" of the 3rd Wisconsin Infantry Brigade, which was recruiting men in accordance with the general call to the colors. Just about that time I was debating with myself as to whether or not I should enlist; the music, evidently, was having the proper effect on me. A few minutes later Arthur Sowards (who was killed in 1917) came along whistling. I called to him and asked him where he was going and why he was not working. He answered back that he "had just enlisted and was going home to pack my belongings." That was the last straw, and that after noon I brought my tools home and stored them away for the last time.

Immediately after supper I went over to the armory, which at that time was located on the second floor of the Robbins Implement Company Building on the corner of South River and Gibson Streets. I presented myself to Captain Richard F. Sortomme, the commanding officer of Company "E", and told him that I wanted to enlist. He, in turn, presented me to Harold Kilboten the Company Clerk, who drew up the necessary papers. I might state here that in those days it was necessary for a person under 21 years of age to have his enlistment papers signed by his father or mother, and a relative or acquaintance, before he could be accepted as a recruit.

Well, that night I came home in pretty high spirits and the all-important papers in my pocket. I decided not to mention my action to anyone until the next morning. I certainly did not sleep much that night, and at 4 A.M. I was up and dressed, but not ahead of my father who generally arose about that time. I told him what I had done and asked him if he would sign my papers. He said he was real glad to know that I had enlisted and felt proud that he could sign my papers for me. As soon as he had done this I went over to Paulson's home and got Oscar out of bed and asked him to sign as a witness, which he immediately did.

So now I was all set for action, and after breakfast, I

went over to the armory and presented my completed papers to Clerk Kilboten. That afternoon several of us were given physical examinations and formally accepted into the service. I was not a full fledged rookie. Sergeant Paul Bernicks, the company Supply Sergeant, furnished me with a rifle, side-arms, and two blankets that same afternoon. They had no uniforms on hand (I got one three weeks later) but since I had a gun I thought I was quite a soldier.

The next two days were spent in giving all the rookies, about twenty-five of us, a few pointers in the elementary foot movements of close order drill, common military courtesies, and certain precautions in the handling of unloaded rifles. We were also told to equip ourselves with all necessary toilet articles, such as soap, towels, combs, and other personal equipage [sic].

The purchasing of these toilet articles was quite a job for those of us who had never attended camp before, and resulted in some humorous incidents. Some of the fellows actually bought night shirts, little realizing that they were inviting some wild experiences by so doing. The folks at home supplied me with towels, soap, comb, and certain other necessities. As far as I could see I figured all I had to buy was handkerchiefs, of which I bought about a dozen. Several days later at Camp Douglas orders were issued to shave every day. I then discovered that I had remembered everything except a razor. Those days I just had to shave about once a week.

Well, at last the big day came, and on June 22nd we entrained for Camp Douglas. Everybody knew, that we would see no real action on the border so there were no tears, or heartbreaks, among the thousands of people assembled at the Northwestern Depot to see us off to camp. My whole family was at the depot to bid me good-bye and good luck. Real army life had started at last.

The picture, shown below, give a good idea of how our departure was celebrated.

1. Richard Krell	6. Henry Lien
2. Myself	7. Oscar Soley
3. Abe Budrow	8. Emil Burkhardt
4. Oscar Olson	9. Frank Boutan
5. Harvey Vermilyea	10. Dick McGrath
11. Carl Ringer	

We pulled into camp shortly after noon and I was given the job of driving stakes for the pyramidal tents. That lasted about two or three hours and by that time the cooks, Arthur Froeling and Arthur Jenks, had supper ready. I was good and hungry, and tired, and my first camp meal of fried potatoes, bacon (sow belly), bread and butter and black coffee tasted great. We all sat around on the ground and ate and had lot of fun together.

After supper we drew bed ticks, without straw, and prepared to spend our first night in camp; that is, the first night for the rookies. Well, it was a wild night. In the first place the mosquitoes were fierce; on top of that the ground felt like rock and my hips started to ache. Then I woke half froze and got up and put on part of my clothes. Just about the time I started to doze-off it was five o'clock and time to get up. I felt as though I hadn't slept a wink for a week. I thought to myself "so this is the army, what an outfit". As days went on, however, I got so that I could sleep just as soundly on the ground as on a soft bed.

The three weeks following our arrival in camp, were spent in learning how to drill, with Sergeant Art (Marcus) Olson – who was killed in 1918 – as our instructor, taking sjort [short] hikes on sandy roads; getting vaccinated against small-pox and various kinds of inoculations. The time went very fast and I was beginning to enjoy the new life as I had never enjoyed anything before.

The second week of July I was given a three day

furlough and I went back to Eau Claire and visited my folks. I had a uniform then and I sure felt proud.

About a week later, sometime during the last week of July 1916, we broke camp and the entire Wisconsin Brigade entrained to San Antonio, Texas with Camp Wilson as our destination. San Antonio, at that time, was headquarters for all border troops.

The train ride was uneventful, except for the changing scenery and increasing heat as we move southward. Once a day we detrained for a few minutes for exercise. After four days and five nights riding we finally reached Camp Wilson and detrained early in the morning of about August first. We were finally arrived at a camp that later proved to make Camp Douglas seem like a vacation ground by comparison.

My first hours at Camp Wilson were spent in exactly the same manner as my first day at Camp Douglas – driving stakes for our tents – and driving stakes in sun-baked Texas gumbo is real manual labor. But by noon the job was finished, and the whole brigade had its camp completed insofar as setting up tents was concerned. Later in the week units from Illinois, (including the 8th Illinois Infantry composed entirely of negroes), Kansas and Oklahoma arrived. In those days we were part of the 12th Infantry Division.

On that first day, after arranging our personal belongings, setting up gun racks, and being detailed to various other camp details, the time came for us to turn in. Well, that first night the only ones that went to bed (we slept on the ground for a couple of months) in the squad tents were those who couldn't find a spot on the roofs of the latrines or bath houses. The camp grounds were alive with scorpions, tarantulas, centipedes, and various other miscellaneous and assorted poison bugs, and we had not had a chance as yet to clean them out. As it turned out, the corporals and sergeants slept on the roofs mentioned, and the privates – including myself – slept on the ground. But no one was bitten, and we all had a lot of fun kidding the non-coms for being so scared of a few bugs.

Our second day in camp fell on Sunday and it gave us all an opportunity to go to town and spend the day sight-seeing. Clarence and I spent the afternoon visiting such places of interest as the Alamo, Breckenridge Park, Hot Springs, the Old mission ruins and the Mexican quarters. I don't believe there is another city in the country so crowded with history and romance as San Antonio.

The month of August was spent mostly in long days of hard drilling and short practice hikes to get us used to the climate and also to gradually harden ourselves.

They were pleasant days, however, and the weather was perfect so we did not mind the hard work in the least. The only thing that bothered us was getting used to drinking alkaline water. Even spring water comes out of the ground milky looking and warm.

September 1916 was a month that I will never forget. Our first real march was to Leon Springs, about thirty miles from San Antonio. We made the hike in two days marching. The camp there lasted about a week, during which we had target practice every day. The place was literally crawling with rattle snakes and scorpions, and although none of the men were bitten we lost quite a number of horse and mules. It was while we were camped there that Company "E" went out on an armadillo hunt and captured two of them for the zoo at Chippewa Falls. (Both of them died shortly after the zoo received them however).

The return march to Camp Wilson was made in two night marches, and we did not fare very well, but we managed to straggle into camp somehow. Camp Wilson was a tough looking place when we pulled in. A cyclone had passed over during our absence and practically all of the mess shacks had the roofs blown off.

Below is a picture of our camp at Luxello
after the storm had passed.

Three weeks later the entire division broke camp and started on the now famous hike to Austin, a distance of ninety miles. The entire hike required three weeks, one week going, one week at Austin (Camp Bowie), and one week returning.

This march saw some real suffering among the men. The days were boiling hot and the nights cold and raw. Hundreds of the men were overcome by the heat and had to be brought in by ambulance or combat wagon. Company "E" had just one bad day; when marching through some arid country near New Braunfels, about fifteen men led by Pat Boyd dropped out of line and lay down in a cool grove. They were just plain tired out. We named the spot "Boyd's Park" and the fellows came in for a lot of kidding when they finally reached camp. Our captain was of the opinion that some of (them) were stalling and handed them a calling down when they straggled in about four hours late.

The one week we spent at Austin was devoted to extended-order drill and wound up with a big sham battle involving the entire division. The working hours were short and it allowed us several hours a day to explore the city. Clarence Cleasby and I signed the guest book in the capitol building and thought we were having a great time. The people of Austin were not very friendly towards the soldiers and we did not regret leaving it when we pulled stakes and started the return trip. They called us Yankees and we called the(m) Rebels, not a very congenial attitude on their part or ours. In no other Texas city did we encounter such an attitude.

The march back to Camp Wilson was uneventful except for the terrific heat and dust and the cold nights. I stood the march real well, and nothing happened until we were actually inside the confines of Camp when I stepped on a sharp stone and broke a small bone in the instep of my right foot. As was his custom, Captain Sortomme said I was stalling, but I paid no attention to him and as soon as I had gotten rid of my pack I went over to the medical corp where Major Moore bound up my foot and fixed me up. I was laid up for about three weeks as a result of this injury. During that time I was assigned to a clerking job at the "Canteen".

Below is a picture taken during the march to Austin.

The months of October and the first three weeks of November were devoted almost entirely to routine drilling and practice hikes to keep in condition. The regular troops in Mexico, had in the meantime, engaged in several skirmishes with bandits, but the situation had, as a whole, quieted down entirely and all U.S. troops were back in the United States again. It is interesting to note that the first and only real battle between bandits and our soldiers resulted for a victory for our side won by a detachment of colored troops.

There was a growing suspicion among the National Guard units that this whole border affair had just been a "test case" to determine exactly just how quickly an army could be mobilized and also to determine what our greatest weaknesses were. In other words, most of us suspected that this was merely a first step towards that which was to come in 1917. Our officers, however, stoutly denied this.

Our last days at Camp Wilson were happy ones as well as busy ones. We rather disliked the idea of leaving San Antonio, a fine city, but we were anxious to get back up north again. Information had come to us that we were to be mustered out at Fort Sheridan, Illinois, and the fact that we would be quartered in regular barracks certainly sounded good to us. We knew too, that we would sleep in real beds instead of on the ground as we had the last five months or so.

About November 20th, 1916, we finally broke camp

and entrained for Fort Sheridan. The trip was uneventful all the way, except for some real celebrating that only soldiers on the way home can properly execute. The thing we all noticed, of course, was that when we got as far north as southern Illinois the green grass had disappeared and in its place patches of snow appeared. However, there was not snow on the ground at Fort Sheridan or the surrounding country. But it was real cold and we felt it keenly as we had been enjoying summer sunshine just four days before.

Our arrival at Fort Sheridan was observed by not having anything to eat for the first day, and nothing but soup for the next week. It can only be faintly imagined what this condition of affairs did to the disposition of the rank and file of the regiment. As we had to live on soup, we refused to stand any formations and there were disturbances of the wildest kind every night. We just laughed at our officers when they attempted to discipline us. Most of us sent home for some substantial food. After about two weeks of this diet we finally got back on a regular basis of feeding, and once more we settled down to business. Thereafter, and until we left for home, everything was peaceful. The days were spent in drilling and getting our equipment in shape, and in the evening we were permitted to take trips to Chicago and the other nearby cities.

Finally, on December 21st, orders came to muster out the unit. We were all given final physical examinations, and in the late afternoon entrained for home stations. This last ride was a regular celebration, and it required all of the tact and patience of our officers to see that the company would be in a presentable condition when we reached Eau Claire.

Our special train pulled in over the Milwaukee Road at about 2 A.M. on December 22nd, 1916, and even at that early hour there were several thousand on hand to greet us. We managed, somehow, to march to the armory and check in our equipment and receive orders to report the next morning for final orders. After many hand-shakes and good-byes among us fellows, we broke ranks and each of us left for the home we had not seen since the last of June.

The next few weeks were spent in informal re-unions and visiting before most of us settled down to the business of finding a job. I secured a painting job with the Dunphy Boat Works on Water Street, and by the last of January 1917 I was working. I worked, however, with a certain uneasy feeling that I, and the other boys, would soon be back in the old uniform. We were back in it sooner than we expected.

WORLD WAR I

The events leading up to the entry of the United States on the side of the Allies are well known to everyone, and the declaration of war against Germany found Company "E" already in the service. The Wisconsin National Guard was called out March 23rd, 1917, and was one of the first Guard units in the country to be so honored.

I received the news in an unusual manner. I was hard at work painting a boat when suddenly Mr. Larsen came bursting into the shop and called: "John - you have to go and fight the Kaiser". I finished the job I was working on and then went into the office and called the armory and told Ira Horel, our 1st Sergeant, that I would report inside of an hour. I then ran back into the shop and bid my friends good-bye. In the meantime Mr. Larsen wrote out my pay check, plus an extra five dollars, shook hands, and I was on my way.

My folks were pretty quiet when I told them the news, and during the next few minutes when I was changing into my uniform very little was said. But then there was not time for long conversation and in the hour's time I was on my way to the armory. Here everything was going full blast; the old border gang was coming in and much time was taken up renewing old acquaintances and reviewing old times. A recruiting office had been set up at once, and before night new recruits were being received.

In two or three days Major Moore, the medical officer arrived, and we were all given medical examination s and inoculations of various kinds. The new recruits were also vaccinated in addition to the inoculations. While all these preliminaries were going on the older men of the company were divided into various details for guard duty, police duty, armory duty, and multitudes of lesser duties within the organization.

I was assigned to guard duty on the two railroad high-bridges in Eau Claire, along with about twenty other men. We stood regular shifts of two hours on and four hours off. This continued until the later part of April when I was assigned to guard duty at Wissota Dam, which was then under construction just two or three miles north of Chippewa Falls.

The picture, below, was taken on that detail.

The guard detail at Wissota was commanded by 2nd Lieutenant Roy Boberg, and the detail itself was about the liveliest gang ever assembled under one roof. It should be remembered, however, that when we were on duty we were all business but when we played we really played. Wissota was a desolate place and to keep it from getting on our nerves we simply had to cut loose once in a while. The work itself was uneventful, and when the time came for us to entrain for Camp Douglas, the middle of August, we were quietly relieved by civilian guards without any ceremony. The one highlight of our stay was our dedication of a flag pole and flag in front of the construction company's office. It is interesting to note that we were fed all this time by the construction company, not by the State.

We were called back to Eau Claire the middle of August 1917, and immediately started preparations for closing the armory and preparing for entrainment and

CO. "E", 127TH INFANTRY. TAKEN AT CAMP DOUGLAS, AUGUST 1917. (PHOTO BY CARL JOHNSON, EAU CLAIRE)

movement to Camp Douglas. This involved only two or three days work, and about the third week of August we were ready to leave Eau Claire, many of the boys for the last time.

On the day of entrainment we were all lined up in front of the armory and given a final inspection. It was a motley looking crowd; over half the outfit consisted of recruits wearing civilian clothes, and of the other half some had new uniforms and some had the old style uniforms. There was no hilarity or celebrating of any kind and everyone was all business.

I spent the last night in Eau Claire with my folks, and instead of eating breakfast downtown with the rest of the outfit, I ate at home. Immediately after eating father took me over to the armory. He and I stood apart from the others and said good-bye to each other. He felt pretty bad and said very little; in his confusion and utter inability to talk he merely said: "good-bye Johnny, keep your feet dry, and God bless you". It was the only time that I ever heard anything bordering on religion spoken by him. Shortly thereafter he went home to get Ella and Minnie and Kenneth, and brought them to the Northwestern Depot where they awaited our arrival for entrainment.

Within five minute after I fell in line with my squad, Captain Sortomme gave the command "forward march" and we were on our way. I never did find out how many thousand were at the depot to see us off - it looked like the entire city. This time we were going to war, and none of us knew if we were ever coming back. Wives and children were kissing their husbands good-bye: brothers and sisters and sweethearts looked tearfully at each other. There was much crying among the older ones, and much cheering and flag waving on the part of the children. All in all it was a wild scene and hard for everyone. Ella, Minnie and Kenneth were crying and saying good-bye over and over, father stood nearby pale and quiet, and Albert who came later, simply shook hands and said very little. I didn't feel so much like celebrating myself.

The train soon pulled in, and in a few minutes we were all aboard and the special pulled out without any further delay. No sooner had we started to move than we were assigned to various camp details so there would be no delay in setting up the camp. Since Camp Douglas is only about a hundred miles from Eau Claire, we reached there in about three hours.

It will be remembered that on my first trip to Camp Douglas in 1916 I was assigned to the job of driving tent stakes; this time I helped unload the tents and other equipment from trucks. Our company was now twice as big as in 1916 and our company street was a good city block long, and the biggest in the regiment. I might mention, at this point, that the army had been reorganized and we were now Company "E" of the 128th Infantry, 32nd Division.

About the second or third day after our arrival, the medical corp started the physical examinations of the new recruits. The examinations they received in Eau Claire were merely preliminaries, but this final examination was the real thing. Out of about seventy-five or eight recruits, possibly twenty were sent back home as unfit. Notable among those sent back was Leonard Hilt, who later made the examination, and was killed, or rather died of injuries received in 1918. However, with the examinations over with we were all set to buckle down to the business of soldiering and to prepare ourselves for rigid training schedules.

The next two weeks or so were spent in drilling and calisthenics to harden us. We worked from 7 A.M. until 4:30 P.M. on the drill field, with one hour for lunch. There were regular guard shifts to stand, and other routine camp duties. On Sundays there were many visitors from Eau Claire, mainly parents come to see how their boys were getting along, and some wives and children, and curious ones.

There were other units waiting to train at Camp Douglas so our stay there was very short, and about the second week of September 1917 we entrained for Camp MacArthur at Waco, Texas. I am reminded here of a letter I received from father while at Camp Douglas. He was then convinced that we would get no further than Camp Douglas. Shortly after we arrived at Waco I received another letter from him in which he was convinced we would not leave the United States because Germany would be licked before then. His conviction was incorrect of course.

The train trip to Waco was rather uneventful, with the usual once-a-day detraining for a little leg stretching. All the way down the line crowds turned out to see the troop trains go through - and also to sell liquor to the soldiers on the sly. Some of the men bought bottles of what they thought was whiskey, but it turned out to be vinegar or colored water in some cases. Outside of little incidents such as that nothing in particular happened. It was my second trip to Texas, over the same route within a year, so it was not new to me.

And, wonder of wonders, there were not tent stakes to drive into the gumbo. The entire camp was already pitched and ready for our arrival. A special detail had been sent down a couple of weeks in advance to prepare the camp. So all we had to do was march in and make ourselves at home. The camp was beautifully located on a great level plain which, shortly before, had been a cotton field. Each regiment had its own drill field in front of its tent area, and the arrangement was perfect. Each regiment also had its own Y.M.C.A. building.

The picture below gives a view of one of these buildings.

After two weeks after our arrival the "Rainbow Division" (42nd) was in the process of formation, comprised of units from every state in the Union. Company "E" of the 127th Infantry, from Fond du Lac, was taken from our Brigade, and Company "E" of the 128th Infantry from Eau Claire took its place. We were now, therefore, Company "E" 127th Infantry. Shortly after this change we were reinforced by about a hundred men from Chippewa Falls who formerly comprised the old Chippewa Separate Company. They were all great fellows and we gave them a hearty welcome and made them feel at home as best we could. Our strength was now about 250 men, and there were no further additions until after suffering our first casualties in France.

Again, as at Camp Douglas, we had numerous physical examinations, and a couple of men were sent home who did not come up to standard.

With all preliminaries now disposed of we settled down to the business of learning how to fight. First call blew at 5 A.M. and by 7 A.M. we were always out on the drill field. We worked until five in the afternoon with night drills and problems nearly every week. Several times we made overnight trips to a system of trenches located several miles from camp where we were put through strenuous maneuvers and also taught how to build barbed-wire entanglements and other defensive devices.

The hardest work put up to us was bayonet practice. To one who had never seen a bayonet course being run over by a class of students, it is a difficult thing to picture or describe. It is positively the hardest kind of exertion to expect from a human being. After running over the course just once we were utterly exhausted. The course was about a block long and interwoven with a series of trenches, hazards and holes. At the end of the course there hung, suspended in frames, a long row of dummies into which we would ram our bayonets, accompanied by much swearing and yelling. On this same course we were taught how to gouge out eyes, how to strangle an enemy by jerking back his helmet, how to extricate a bayonet that had become lodged in a bone, how to smash a jaw with a blow from the rifle butt, how to cause an internal injury by a smash in the abdomen, how to sever a windpipe and various other niceties, all of which was required of an efficient soldier.

By this time we were in dead earnest; how to kill a man and at the same time preserve ourselves became the order of the day. We tried to become good scholars in this new school.

Interspersed with bayonet work and training was considerable target practice, and concerning which, I became a pretty fair shot. I always liked that phase of army life because it gave a little chance to hold contests among ourselves. Naturally, since the rifle is the infantyman's principal weapon, we were anxious to become proficient in its use. We used a Springfield rifle, calibre [sic] 30-30.

This sort of training continued every day until January 2nd, 1918, when we left for Camp Merritt, New Jersey.

The weather was actually hot when we left Waco, and when we reached Englewood, 36 hours later, near which Camp Merritt was located, it was nearly ten below zero, the same sort of contrast as when we arrived at Fort Sheridan in 1916.

We reached Camp Merritt at about sun-down, and immediately were assigned to our barracks. These buildings were comfortable, well heated, two story affairs, and each building accommodated two platoons of infantry, or one-half a company. They were well equipped with running water and heating systems and we thought they were great. They were painted green with white trimmings.

Well, we were fed shortly after arriving and after supper the first guard detail was named. I escaped this duty as I was acting as First Lieutenant John Martin's orderly and working for him exempted me from any additional company duties or work. The men chosen for guard had to dress like Eskimos to stand the cold, and then they nearly froze.

The camp had a liberty theatre, a Y.M.C.A., a K. of C. building and Salvation Army Hut to furnish amusement and a more homelike atmosphere for the boys, and they were well accommodated at all times. These different agencies put on a show nearly every night, as well as conducting religious services and providing club rooms of a sort. The theatre ran regular movies for an admission price of five cents. There were also libraries provided. It was while we were at Camp Merritt that I made the acquaintance of a Mr. Tenhaf, a Y.M.C.A. man, who gave me the little flag that I still have and treasure. He had a marvelous tenor voice and was loved by all for his beautiful singing and genuine kindness and understanding. He wanted to go overseas but could not on account of his age. He also was our Y man at Waco, Texas.

While stationed here I was promoted to corporal.

About the fifteenth of February orders came to prepare to embark. It caught Company "E" at a bad time because the second platoon, consisting of about seventy men, was quarantined due to a case of scarlet fever. As things turned out, they sailed about three weeks later and were sent to England, where they remained until the end of the war doing special guard duty as Military Police - "MP's".

The orders to sail did not cause any confusion, but it most certainly excited everyone because it meant that we were going into something which might mean our lives, and every man did his work in a sort of a daze. There were hurriedly written letters home, last minute telegrams, and even a couple of long distance telephone calls went through. All of our baggage was picked up by trucks and brought to Hoboken for loading onto the ship, and all we kept with us was our regular equipment such as our service packs.

We were loaded into trains at Englewood, New Jersey, and were transported the short distance to Hoboken. We marched through the crooked streets of the city singing and whistling and wise-cracking, much to the amusement of the younger people who turned out to see us march through. Many of the older people, especially old men and women, who realized what could happen had tears in their eyes when we went by and it was noticed by many of the fellows. Now we were really on the way out and over.

After a hike of about four or five blocks we reached the pier, and there lying in her berth loomed up the great transport the U.S.S. George Washington - formerly a German liner - that was to take us overseas. None of us had ever seen a big ship before, and the sight of this huge eight-hundred foot boat gave us a real thrill. As we march aboard a delegation from a Jewish Welfare agency presented each of us with a real useful gift and bid each and every soldier good-bye and good luck. They were the last regular American civilians that we were to see for a year and a half.

The above picture gives a good idea as to the size
of our transport.

It did not take the outfit long to get on board, in
a couple of hours there were 7700 soldiers on the ship.
We were immediately assigned to bunks and our Company drew Deck F. Each of us also drew a meal ticket because with all those thousands on board to feed the food
had to be well and closely conserved. The next couple
of hours were spent exploring, and soon we were under
way. Fritz Daub got seasick the instant he set foot on deck
and when he reached his bunk he stayed there until we
reached Brest. He vowed that he would never cross the
ocean again until they built a bridge across. But he broke
his vow and came home again and was even more seasick
than he was on the way over.

As we steamed slowly down the East River, tugs, and other harbor craft, tooted a salute to us and dipped their craft flags, as was their custom when transports were going out. When we passed the Statue of Liberty all hands that were on deck stood at attention as the band played the Stars [sic] Spangled Banner, and then broke into wild cheering. In a matter of an hour we were on the open sea. Later our ship was joined by about ten other transports, together with a convoy of several battle cruisers and destroyers (which we were all glad to see).

About the funniest sight a person can hope to see is a couple of thousand seasick land-lubbers, and we sure had them. Even the mention of food emptied their stomachs, in fact all they had to do was think about food. I was not seasick but I had a splitting headache for a couple of days. But by the second day we all felt fine and the ride became a real pleasure. At least everyone was in good condition by the time Washington's birthday came around, when the ship's crew put on a big feed for us.

The look-out sighted a submarine when we were about ten days out, but after much heavy cannonading and maneuvering on our part the thing disappeared. Some said that our guns sunk it. While all this was going on we stood at our assigned stations in case the order should come to abandon ship. I should say that we "shook" at our stations because everyone was plenty upset. That was the only scare of the entire trip across, and that was

30

enough for anyone. The transport President Grant broke her rudder which caused about a week's delay to the fleet in mid-ocean, but after twenty one days of sailing we finally sighted the coast of France on the morning of March 3rd, 1918. As we drew closer to land we could distinguish queer looking trains and buildings - and what a thrill.

FRANCE

We anchored well out in the stream because the harbor was too shallow to handle our ship at the pier. Little tugs with high funnels were scooting around our boat helping us to get into position for unloading. We could now get a good view of the city which is built partly on the side of a hill sloping down towards the sea. The city of Brest is a beautiful place from a distance, but a filthy place when you get into it.

In the meantime power barges were pulling up alongside and we prepared to disembark. That solid ground sure looked good to us and we were anxious to get onto it after three weeks on the ocean. I might state here that the transport President Grant was sunk on its return trip to the U.S. Well, by the time we had gotten our things together, and our packs strapped on, it was time to step on the barge and head for the shore. This required only a few minutes and inside a half an hour we were on shore and preparing to entrain for Bordaux, our first oversea[s] camp.

Our first glimpse of a French troop train was a real jolt. It consisted of a long string of tiny freight cars, mounted on four wheels. Each car had this legend painted on its side: "40 Hommes et 8 Chevaux" - meaning 40 men or 8 horses. In other words they were used for transporting either horses or men. But they were not so bad, and we piled in, 40 men in a car. The train was pulled by a wheezy looking high wheeled engine with a brass boiler that periodically let funny peeps through its whistle. We got a big laugh out of the whole thing.

It didn't take long to entrain and after much shouting and hand signaling on the part of the train crew we were under way. It was Springtime and the country-side was beautiful. We all just sat and watched the passing scenery. I don't believe there is anything as picturesque as a rural French community with its quaintly dressed, wooden shod people. In this part of the country there was no sign of war, except for the presence of soldiers in some of the towns, and we thoroughly enjoyed the ride. Our only discomfort came at night because there was not room to lay down and we had to try to sleep sitting with our legs crossed. When our legs started to ache we simply stood up to stretch them. And besides that the nights were cold and damp. During each night, however, for the four nights we thus rode, we were each given a small ration of rum, mixed with hot coffee to warm us up. This ration, distributed gratis by the French Army, served to warm us up a little and possibly prevented sickness to a great extent. The days however were pleasant and we all enjoyed it immensely.

The evening of March 8th we pulled into camp near the city of Bordeaux. It was a barrack camp and not a bad place at all. Events were now moving rapidly. This was not to be a long stopover and aside from an epidemic of mumps in the regiment, nothing of any import happened.

We were all given a chance to see the city of Bordeaux with its beautiful statuary, famous wineries and great fountains. Here also we got out first real glimpse of French troops in their blue and red uniforms. Here also we saw countless numbers of French veterans crippled and blinded from the war. We also saw orphaned children and widowed wives and bereaved parents, and it brought to us the sudden realization that soon we would be taking our own chances in the trenches.

On Easter Sunday, March 31, 1918, we again entrained and were transported to St. Sulpice, a little closer to the lines. Here the 127th assisted in building new barracks and roads, and life was not pleasant for a time. However, our stay was short, and the first part of April we again entrained, this time to Alsace-Lorraine, and to a small village by the name of Leuchey. We were quartered in barn sheds, and vacant buildings of all kinds. Just the Second Battalion was quartered here. The village is about five miles from the nearest railroad.

For the first week we spent our time cleaning up the town, such as moving manure piles from the street, draining away stagnant water, and in general put the town in a sanitary condition for the first time in perhaps two hundred years. The natives actually rebelled at the clean-up. I did not think that humans could live in such filth. We also re-named all the streets to suit ourselves, giving them such names as Barstow Street, Grand Avenue, Eau Claire Street and the like. Captain Sortomme was town Marshall and he soon had things in fine shape and the people hardly recognized their own city. With this work completed we settled down to a ten hour day schedule at open and trench warfare drill and brushed up on our technique of soldiering again. The weather was perfect, and we accomplished a lot and felt that we were ready for the front lines.

On May 18th we again pulled stakes and left for the front lines near Lutran. As we drew closer to our destination we could distinguish occasional rumbles of heavy gun fire, and when we did reach Lutran there was no mistaking of what we had heard. On clear days we could distinguish machine gun fire and rifle fire. We had at last reached the theatre of operations and everything was done differently, and there was much secrecy. The streets were camouflaged and at night no lights were permitted to show in the open. There was a perceptible change in our ranks too; the boys of yesterday were now serious faced men who talked nothing but war and their duties. It was while here that Chaplain Gustav Stearns conducted his first service in a zone of action. Our entire stay was devoted to drilling of the most intensive kind. A French Sergeant was also assigned to us for technical advice.

Shortly after our arrival at Lutran it was my good fortune to be appointed to the Gas School at Gondre-court, located well back from the zone of action, along with Captain Sortomme. We left together and were gone about three weeks. It was a wonderful school, conducted by the British Army, and upon completion of the course each student was considered to be a full fledged gas instructor. It was hard work but extremely interesting and instructive. One of my school mates was Hank Gowdy of the New York Giants baseball team - a fine man. Upon graduation each of us was presented with a complete new uniform and sent back to instruct our units in the art of gas defense. Captain Sortomme put me in charge of all our gas equipment such as masks, horns, signal apparatus, shovel and repair supplies and incidentals. I enjoyed my new work, and as a reward I was assigned to Company headquarters.

About the middle of June we left Lutran, with its

pleasant surroundings, for the trenches at P.C. Stockette. I never saw such excitement; the orders to move up had come unexpectedly and sort of caught us unawares. But we straightened out quickly and we were soon on the march to the front - albeit a quiet one. We entered the trenches at night, so the Germans would not see us, relieving a French unit. It was an eery [errie] proceeding and hearts pounded hard. The Germans across no-mans' land evidently were suspicious because they sent up rockets every few minutes and we would have to drop down on our stomachs. The relief was completed in an hours time and when daylight arrived we found ourselves in trenches built by an enemy who had intended to stay. Some of them were reinforced with logs, and the dug-outs were about ten feet deep and built of concrete and steel. The place was wet and muddy and literally over-run with rats the size of small cats who were fed by decaying corpses lying out there in front of us. The scene around us was indescribable; trees with only stumps remaining, shell holes six feet deep and twelve feet wide, and a churned up conglomeration of barbed wire, branches, bits of clothing, pieces of wagons, helmets, skeletons, and every conceivable thing that could make a perfect picture of a destroyed civilization. And over it all larks, and robin, and thrushes sang cheerily.

I went out with several raiding parties the next week or two, but the only thing we accomplished was getting a good view of the enemy trenches and the general lay of the land, and left marks to let them know we had been there; we also picked up a couple of mauser pistols. It was a nerve wracking experience, crawling and sneaking across no-mans' land in the pitch blackness hardly daring to breath or whisper, and where a cough would have meant a barrage. However, we suffered no casualties and we really enjoyed the raids because they seemed comparatively safe although we sort of hoped that we would have a skirmish to kind of "break us in".

For several days our listening port sentries had heard the Boche cutting wire over to our left, near the position held by our third platoon under the command of Ira Horel. This meant only one thing, they were coming over to attack us soon. Captain Sortomme immediately had supplies of ammunition and grenades sent up to Lieutenant Horel and his men while they waited for the inevitable. I was stationed at Company Headquarters and had a wonderful opportunity to observe preparations.

Well, about the second of July it came. Near midnight all hell broke loose at once. For nearly an hour the Germans laid down a barrage of our position, and our field artillery replied in kind after signal. Then suddenly all was quiet for an instant; we knew that they had come over; then our machine guns opened up with a terrific fire. In our dugout there was feverish activity. We quickly buckled on our side-arms and masks, and stood with rifles in hand waiting to be called - but we were not called. We waited thus for possibly half an hour during which we could hear the fighting with rifles and grenades, up near our third platoon position, and the steady rattle of machine guns. It was a terrific suspense for us, we knew that men were dying - perhaps our own buddy - and here we stood waiting. Outside our dugout men were screaming and groaning and all we could do was hope for them and wait for the order to reinforce the third platoon.

In another instant all was quiet - a ghastly quiet. We knew it was over with, and in the dim morning light we raced outside. The first man we saw was private Howell who was walking his post with his left arm torn out by the socket and spurting blood like a faucet. A couple of men grabbed him to stop the flow of blood and get him to an aid station. He was faithful to his oath beyond all question, and some of the men cried just at the sight of him. We ran up the trench and found Ole Slining dead in a pool of blood. Further up the line men were lying wounded and gasping, and a dead German perforated with bayonet wounds lay in another spot. The wounded were quickly put on stretchers and taken to the hospital in ambulances. We lost only two killed however. It had been a bitter hand to hand fight but the Boche took no prisoners and were driven out and the first fight of the war for the 32nd division was won by a small detachment of our own boys.

We learned later that the Germans lost about twenty men in this big raid. Just the night before the raid, Ole

Slining, who was suffering from rheumatism said that he couldn't stand the pain much longer and would just as soon die. Well, his wish was granted but we all felt badly about it because he was a prince of a man. He was buried with full honors. I do not recall the name of the other one who was killed, he was a replacement from some western division.

On the 19th of July we were relieved by a French unit of the French 47th and we marched back into the city of Dannemarie, a place of about 20,000 population. Here we rested for a couple of days before starting active training again. Our first fight, our baptism of fire as we called it, had not unnerved us in the least and we were in fine fettle both physically and mentally and were all anxious to take another crack at the Kaiser. General Hahn, our Division commander, held a parade in honor of our third platoon, and marched them up and down in front of the rest of the outfit and also in front of some French troops. It was a great day for Company "E" and a fitting climax to our stay in Alsace-Lorraine, a "quiet sector".

I neglected to mention that a few days prior to the raid, described above, that private Earl McGinnis was taken prisoner during a small daylight raid. He spent the balance of the war in Germany working on a farm. He was not an alert soldier, and we were not surprised to learn of his capture although we felt sorry for him of course. At the same time they captured McGinnis they pitched a bomb into a dugout that Harold Johnson was occupying and it wounded him badly in a dozen places. He spent the balance of the war in the hospital but came out of it in good shape.

After a few days spent at Dammemarie, a fine well laid out little city, we were marched to the town of Retzweiller further back of the lines. This too, was a fine little place, but in place of billets we pitched pup tents and set up a regular camp. Our time was spent in drilling and practicing trench warfare. There were some wild scenes in the city at night, but as a whole most of the men conducted themselves with pretty good control of their thirst. We had a feeling that we would not have many more good times over here and our officers were good enough to let the outfit break loose a little. During the months prior to this time my bunking partner had been Albert Hopland from Osseo, Wisconsin, a fine fellow both physically and morally. I mention this because of later events.

On July 29th we received orders to go up to the big Western front, on the Marne River, beyond Belleau Woods and Chateau Thierry where the American regular army was fighting to drive back the Boche and where the French were getting the worst of it at the great second battle of the Marne. The news was received with wild cheering but inwardly we all felt that most anything was possible now. We were given an inspection to see that all our equipment was in shape and then put into trains and headed towards Paris and the battle front.

Enroute we passed several hospital trains filled with wounded soldiers, and as we drew closer to the front there were endless trains of ambulances both motor and horse drawn. We also passed lines of artillery on the way up to the front.

We detrained a few miles from Chateau Thierry and marched up through the city and into the outskirts. Everyone and everything was in the wildest confusion. This once beautiful city was a smashed up shambles, and the surrounding country simply did not resemble anything made by nature. There was terrific artillery fire that was absolutely continuous - an unending roar that is hard to describe. Hundreds of thousands of French and Americans were fighting and straining every resource to hold back the Boche until re-inforcements and replacements should arrive and help them. We met any number of French soldiers, on special detail back of the lines shouting: "fini la guerre, fini Paris". They figured they were beaten and the war nearly over. It was in fact a critical period of war.

The next day found us in bivouac just back of the line and in rear of Reddy Farm, (a private estate) where we awaited orders for advance. We had already seen some fighting in the trenches, but I thought to myself that our experience there was not even a good skirmish compared to the possibilities here. All around us there were countless hundreds of dead Americans, French, and Germans, killed perhaps a couple of days before and still unburied. Some were mangled beyond belief; some with heads missing ; some with faces shot away; many with gaping holes clear through their bodies; many disemboweled with their entrails strewn alongside; some with just a little blue cross on their forehead; some with eyes closed; some with eyes open staring crazily into space. I walked about this ghastly area with unbelieving eyes, then turned from the sickening sight and breathed a prayer for my own Company "E". Men that govern the affairs of nations should witness scenes like this, and if they would there would be no more war.

The night was a hectic one, the artillery fire would not allow much sleep and there was alarm after alarm. Hopland and I finally got up and rolled our packs and waited for daylight. We sat and talked for several hours. He had a peculiar feeling that he was not going to live much longer and mentioned it over and over. When daylight finally came the firing grew more intense, and we were told a counter-attack was to be made shortly by the Americans and French - including our division.

Captain Sortomme called us together informally and told us in effect: "In an hour or so we will meet the Boche, some of us will not come out of it but I know you will make a good account of yourselves; good luck, and may God go with you". He then formed the company and we moved out through Reddy Farm with fixed bayonets and determined, but hammering hearts. The day was blistering hot and sultry and with a forty-five pound pack on our backs it was painful walking. But we were hard as nails and ready to go. We were all given two-hundred rounds of ammunition in addition to that carried in our belts. I also filled my pockets with ammunition for my pistol. The instant we reached the jumping off point and deployed for the attack the Germans opened fire. We advanced towards them in great waves, running full tilt with bayonets glinting in the sun. When about six-hundred yards from them we dropped and opened fire. French observers said they had never seen such intense rifle fire, which with the German firing and own machine guns and artillery made the most terrific din that can be imagined. There were possibly a million troops in action in this second battle of the Marne that was to mark the turning point of the war.

The Boche were holding a strip of woods directly in front of Company "E". After firing about twenty-five rounds we got the signal to advance again and we rose and ran forward, firing from the hip. This time the Germans found the range and were firing point blank at us. I saw Kick Johnson (of Eau Claire) grab his stomach and sink to the ground fatally wounded, together with about ten more of our company. As we slowly advanced I stumbled upon Bill McSorlie with blood spurting from his left arm that was mangled from a direct hit. Captain Sortomme was starting to bandage it and as I came up he had me finish the job and put on a tourniquet. Leaving him I rejoined the company and started firing again. This time we fired so long and rapidly that our hands blistered from our hot rifles. We advance again, this time right to the edge of the woods, and prepared for a final charge. Peter Frendall, who was next to me, was shot through the neck, blood spouted from the back of his neck and through his mouth. Again I bandaged and let the patient lay. Further along was Lieutenant Martin with his face covered with blood from a wound that had nearly scalped him. Alfred Johnson (from Eleva) lay on his back, his face white as snow, and between his eyes a little blue cross, and a bunch the size of an apple in the back of his head where his brains were oozing out, and he was still conscious and able to talk feebly.

We got the order to charge and with bayonets set we tore into the woods yelling and firing from the hip. A German rifleman was shooting at Captain Sortomme and missing every shot; I lunged at him as he started to shoot at me. I missed him the first time but at the second lunge I caught him in the throat and my bayonet slit his wind-pipe; his eyes gave a sudden bulge and he nearly fell on me as he toppled over. He was about my age - and for an instant it sickened me. Just ahead of me lay "Spud" Griffin with a cut in his side; near by George Berg lay with a wound in his groin, and Leslie Weese stood back of a tree pitifully trying to bandage his right hand that was nearly torn off by a burst of machine gun fire. In the meantime we drove the Boche out, but the losses of both sides were terrific. German prisoners were pressed into service as stretcher bearers. We captured a number of machine guns, which we immediately spiked, and other miscellaneous items. The ground was littered with dead and dying and our first-aid men were taxed to the breaking point. I ran back to a first-aid station with Frank Cole who was shot through the side. The floor was slippery with blood and I stood in puddles of it. But we had won - and as night fell we withdrew to Reddy Farm, our base, to re-form and stand roll-call.

Early the next morning, before moving out again to continue the drive, we had roll call. Herman Foss, our first sergeant, called the roll. Over a hundred men were missing out of two-hundred and fifty, and when he reached the end of the roll he fainted, overcome by the awful losses of the day. He had been sick for a few days and the combination of the two was more than he could stand. My pal and bunk mate Albert Hopland, had been instantly killed and there was hardly a man who had not lost a friend. This night (at Reddy Farm) I had to stay up in the court yard and guard for gas. It was hard work because the air was heavy with powder smoke and dust, it was stifling hot, and we were being shelled by long range heavy artillery. All through the night our own artillery laid down an unending barrage to prepare the way for our next advance. When daylight came I was pretty tired after being on my feet for twenty-four hours - sixteen hours of steady fighting and eight hours of guard work. At about four in the morning of July 31, 1918, we moved out.

The Germans had found that they were unable to hold their position of yesterday, and, leaving many of their dead lying about, they were rapidly retreating. They even left guns and wagons and supplies in their haste to get away from the terrific attack. The wheat field over which we attacked on the 30th was a shambles. Dead were strewn about in heaps, huge shell holes dotted the country, and one could not possibly imagine that only a few hours before wheat was growing here. There were, however, the ever present poppies blooming in places. We found two instances of machine gunners - German - chained to their guns and the gunner lying dead alongside. We found several bayonets with saw-teeth, explosive bullets, and other evidences of unorthodox warfare.

In the meantime our artillery hammered away incessantly and we were trying to catch up with an enemy who was on the run. We caught up with him once and deployed for action but Heinie changed his mind and started to run again. When we were lying on our stomachs ready to fire they also shelled us. A shell burst so close behind me that the concussion partly jerked my right arm out of joint. Frank Lawler had his face torn open; Bill Bell was drilled clear through; John Wicklund was killed outright; Michael Meuli was blown to atoms by a direct hit; George Killian was killed outright, and a number of other Company "E" boys were either killed or wounded. One started to run to the rear and I shot him through the hand. But we kept up the advance, and for three days and nights it continued without us having either food, water, or sleep. We ran out of water and for a couple of days we went without drinking. Men actually walked in their sleep. Mike Burke (a replacement from New York and a good friend of mine) led me for nearly half an hour in an attempt to rouse me. We pursued the retreating German Army so closely that at times we could hear them yelling at their horses.

On one point, on the Orcq River, I lay with a detachment on an observation post; it became evident that our commander had lost track of us. I sent a man back to get a message through and we never saw him again. Ralph Simcox who was going mad pleaded with me to get them out of the hole, but I was without orders and could not leave. Some boy, from another outfit who was with us, had both legs smashed from a direct hit and Bert Kappus and I carried him downstream for nearly three miles to a first-aid station. At one place we had to crawl through a culvert with the stretcher balanced on our shoulders to keep him out of the water. We made our way back to the outfit on post and shortly afterwards received word, by runner, to join the rest of the company as the advance was about to proceed.

GAS ATTACK

We marched and crawled nearly all day and in the blackness of the night of August 5th, 1918, we reached the outskirts of Fismes on the Vesle river. Here the German army had dug in for a defense. They laid down one of the most devastating barrages I ever saw, and the exploding shells and rockets lighted up a hectic scene. Company "E" had been reduced to less than twenty-five men. Near mid-night a shell exploded right in front of me as I was crossing the road and the force of the explosion threw me clear across the road and into a ditch where I lay in a daze, bleeding through the mouth and unable to move. I could hear men pleading for water and calling for doctors to help them. A gas attack came over and in my stunned condition I breathed in the poisoned air unknowingly. The next thing I knew I was in a first-aid station and faithful Mike Burke standing over me. Andrew Kleppin (from Eau Claire) pinned a hospital tag on me, and the battle of the Marne was over as far as I was concerned. The aid station, was a partly demolished church, was filled to overflowing with wounded Americans, French and Germans.

At daybreak they loaded us into ambulances and took us to a railroad station where we were placed aboard an English hospital train for transportation to a base hospital. I lay between white sheets for the first time since August 1917. A nurse brought me a cup of hot tea which I swore was the best thing I ever tasted. In about five hours we arrived at Base Hospital 49 near Neufchateau and were carried in stretchers into the wards assigned to us. My stomach burned and ached and I could not eat anything except liquid food for about two weeks. But after careful treatment for four weeks I was ready to leave the hospital and go back to my outfit again. The treatment of gas cases was not understood by even the best doctors and we had no assurance that we would long survive. I felt pretty good, however, and, although a little weak, I was anxious to see Company "E" again and the old gang.

I was equipped with a new uniform, shoes, helmet, and other requirements, and put on board a passenger train with about a hundred other soldiers discharged from the hospital. We rode for possibly twenty-four hours until we reached the end of the safety limit where we detrained and started to hitch-hike back to the lines and our respective outfits. By the next night we could hear the firing again, and before the next night we were back with our companies again and got in the tail end of the Juvigny fight. But the division was relieved the next morning and we went back of the lines for a ten days rest - which was our only breathing space of the war.

I hardly recognized Company "E" with its nearly two-hundred replacements, but during the next few days quite a few of the old bunch returned from various hospitals. I learned that Carl Wanger and Arthur Sowards had been killed, together with some of the newer men. Our company commander was now Captain Charles S. Normington, Captain Sortomme having been sent back to the States as an instructor. Captain Normington promoted me to the rank of line sergeant within three days after my arrival from the hospital. During the short rest I gave a couple of lectures on "gas defense" for the new men. After about ten days rest we received orders to proceed to the Argonne forest, across the Meuse River, where an all-American drive on the famous Hindenburg Line, "The Kriemhild Stellung", was about to start. The line had never been broken by allied troops and the 32nd division was going in as special shock troops.

This time we did not entrain as we were too close to the front line. Instead we were transported in trucks as far as they dared to take us. We had trucks of three different armies, French, English, and American, and we noticed that most of the drivers were Japanese soldiers. We were packed into the trucks as tightly as possible, and started off. It was a hilarious division that rode that day, and although the ride was humpy and bumpy, there was much singing and yelling and we had a great time during this new method of transportation. The new replacements were especially hilarious, they had seen no action as yet or they would not have been quite so peppy. When we got within range of enemy long-range guns we piled out and started marching. We marched through a country whose cities had been actually blown off the earth. Nothing but shell holes and debris marked the places where there were once peaceful, thriving cities. Gradually we marched into the actual zone of action.

Overhead the sky was filled with battle planes; the spectacle of seeing a couple of squadrons of airplanes engaged in a fight to the death cannot be described, it has to be seen to be understood. For the first time since the entry into the war we had ample protection from the air. At one place, near Romagne, two French observation balloons were observing enemy movements from their high place when suddenly out of nowhere two Boche planes dove on them and set them both afire. The French pilots of the balloons bailed out and floated safely to earth with the Germans trying to hit them. The balloons burst into flames and fell about half a mile from where we were assembled. It was a thrilling escape on the part of the Frenchmen and a neat job on the part of the Boche.

Well, we finally took up our position for the advance and our jumping-off place was an apple orchard just outside the remains of a small village. German planes had been watching us closely and a few shells had dropped near us as they attempted to find the range. Our guns evidently had the range because the firing was continuous, and we could hear our long-range shells whistling overhead. Very shortly the Boche too found the range and before long their shells were screaming into us and all around us. Although there were some casualties the loss was trivial considering the location and not much attention was paid to their firing. The new men were having some uneasy moments and we older ones noticed that they needed no lessons in learning how to "dig-in." But they held up fine and aside from two or three there was no case of shock. The order came, and we started a slow advance. The first obstacle was a river to be forded and as the enemy was dropping shells with increasing regularity it was a ticklish job. However, we got across without any loss, and were soon well on the way to the actual battle front. We slowly advanced up hills and through valley and across level stretches, and when darkness came we were within calling distance of the outfit we were to relieve which I think was the 91st division and a portion of the 5th division. We had a terrible time getting through some old barbed-wire in the blackness, but around midnight we had completed the relief and taken up our position preparatory for the attack on the next morning. It was now October 4th, 1918, and the morale of the men was wonderful, especially since we had just learned that Turkey and Bulgaria had given up the fight.

Around two in the morning, of October 5th, our artillery started the barrage. I thought I had seen some great French firing, but it could not be compared to this American firing. All forms of guns were in action, light and heavy artillery, long-range guns, field artillery, and even airplanes dropping great bombs got into action. The roar simply cannot be imagined, and as far as the eye could see there was nothing but the black smoke of bursting shells and the resulting flashes of fire and flying deris [sic]. It was absolutely continuous, and from our position we could see the German position, on a hill in front of us, gradually being plowed under. We knew that no person could possibly live through such a hell, and when our artillery outfits had demolished the position it moved its fire further back. When the entire territory had been combed thus, our gunners began dropping shells all over, regardless of range. First a shell would drop near the Boche line, then in front of it, then to one side, then way in the rear. It was nick-named the "crazy barrage", and we learned from some captured Germans that in all their experience they had never seen or heard a barrage so intense and deadly. It literally blew the Boche out of their positions. In the meantime, of course, they were laying position until the time for attacking should come. They were firing at us point-blank and were displaying the best marksmanship I had seen on their part.

The illustration, below, gives a pretty fair idea of how barbed-wire is arranged.

There was not much for us to do except to stay in our position and wait orders for the attack which would come as soon as the barrage was completed. The battle now consisted of an artillery duel, and to attempt an advance would be useless. We suffered numerous casualties, the most serious of which was that of a man named Hennicke who had both feet blown off at the ankles and bled to death in an hour.

Around six in the morning the order came to step out of position, deploy for action, and prepare to attack the hill in front of us. It was not now occupied but the Boche would defend it with artillery and the advance promised to be a difficult one. The terrain over which we had to advance was very hilly and no matter how we advanced the Boche had a good view of us. Our third platoon, under Sergeant Downs was the first to leave concealment and form for action. No sooner had they stepped out of the woods than Sergeant Downs was drilled through the side and lay on the ground gasping and calling for help. A couple of his men grabbed him and dragged him back to where we were where he was given first aid and left lying there for the medical men to pick up later. A moment later the entire brigade stepped out, and this was the signal for the Germans to open up with a hot artillery fire. But we advanced in huge waves, with bayonet fixed and rifles cocked for action. There evidently were not enemy infantry-men in front of us because there was no rifle or machine-gun fire, only light artillery firing at us point blank and raising havoc with our alignment. But the advance never wavered for a moment, everyone sensed the ultimate victory and nothing could stop us now.

WOUNDED

The artillery fire from the German lines, as I said before, was something terrific, and there was practically no place where the shells were not dropping from and which there was no escape on account of the open nature of the country. A number of Company "E" men went stark mad and became raving maniacs and just ran with the rest, hollering and yelling until they would fall in a dead faint. It is a pitiful thing to watch a shell-shocked man trying to find a place to hide from the screaming shells and their deafening explosions; it is not a case of fear, but simply nerves that will not hold up. The majority of us were nearly deaf and had to yell in each others ears to make ourselves heard. We steadily advanced, and still there was no rifle fire, nothing but artillery now firing from in back of the hill in front of us. We had already gone through the

Hindenburg line and were pushing the Boche into territory that they had held since the war began and we were moving up so fast that they could not get set for a counter-attack. In the midst of the awful firing airplanes were dropping bombs on us and strafing us with machine-guns, but the advance could not be stopped. Company "E" was now starting to have numbers of casualties. Joseph Loicca had the top of his head cut clear off just above the eyes, Carl Ringer came running with his arm sticking straight out behind him from being jerked out of joint by the concussion of an exploding shell. There were many other Company "E" boys lying about on the ground pale and helpless waiting for doctors to bandage them and stop the flow of blood. The ground was simply littered with dead German soldiers who had been caught in our artillery fire and they attempted to reach their rear. What little remained of one-time roads was blocked with dead and dying horses, smashed wagons, smashed artillery limbers with dead drivers in some of the seats. The attack was so swift that nothing could escape. Finally, about mid-way up the hill, a huge shell burst about ten feet from where I stood, there was a peculiar whistle and a sudden burning in my left arm. I could feel that the arm was broken and looking down saw blood streaming from my hand and a splinter of steel stuck through my coat. I hollered at James McGee, our bugler, to tell Captain Normington that I was heading for a first-aid station and would be back shortly, although I did not see how I could, I wanted to try to set an example for my platoon for new men so that they would not get panicky. As I was about to start back Clarence Cleasby came on the run, he had been hit just back of the ear and was nearly knocked out, and we made our way back together. It was harder to get back than it was to advance because the Boche were laying down a fire on our rear guard, evidently to block the bringing up of supplies. Horse drawn artillery units were going up on the gallup [sic], together with great columns of infantry, and the enemy artillery was unable to stop them.

Back in a first-aid station I had the splinter removed from my arm, splints put on, and was sent still further back to a collecting depot. In the aid station some terrible sights greeted us. Several Company "E" boys were in there badly hurt, and one of them, whoses [sic] name I have forgotten, had his lower jaw completely shot away and it made a grewsome [sic] picture to see his upper teeth exposed and him trying to talk to us. I have often wondered since as to whether or not he lived. Doctors were working stripped to the waist and nearly worn out. A major by the name of Watson was in charge, and he was a marvelous surgeon.

I was put aboard a truck, with several other wounded men, and we were on our way to the hospital again. Some of the fellows in there had broken legs and every time the truck would hit a bump they would scream and yell something fierce. We rode for perhaps three hours before we reached a train station. At this point we were all given shots against lock-jaw, but bandages were not changed. We thought we would be sent to a base hospital right away, but we were held here three or four days waiting for transportation. In the meantime maggots were beginning to work into my wounded arm, and it ached and "drew" pretty bad. By the time I finally did get to a base hospital there were black streaks up and down my forearm and gangerine [sic] had set in. The doctors cut away the infected part and then poured iodine into the hole. I fainted dead away and when I came to my arm was all freshly bandaged and set with new splints and felt pretty good. I do not recall the name of the hospital but it was either number 51 or 59, and was located near the city where Joan of Arc was born. I believe the name of the city was Baziolle.

The hospital was a fine institution all except the food, which was poor. We had soup for nearly every meal and our only implement with which to serve ourselves was a fork. We had a lot of fun about it and since we were not sick we could do a lot of exploring around. This hospital contained nothing but surgical cases and we were not confined to beds, that is those of us who were not injured internally or did not have injured legs or feet and so on. After four weeks here, I presented myself to Doctor Watson (Captain Watson) who was in charge, and asked permission to rejoin my company at the front. He asked me why, and I said "for two reason; one is to get a square meal again, and the other is because I want to get back to the old gang". I was nearly court-martialed for running down the meals but I got permission to have the office hand me my release. My arm was still bandaged but it was pretty well healed and the danger was over with and I felt fit and sound.

Once again I was given railroad tickets and put aboard a train with a few hundred other soldiers. We again rode to the end of the danger line and then left the train to hitch-hike back to our outfits. This time we had a hard time locating our regiments, and we were on "our own" for over a week. No provision was made for feeding us and we had to eat whatever we could find. Chester Peterson and I struck out alone and we had some interesting experiences. We went through some partly destroyed towns that were absolutely deserted. Just about the time we were getting so hungry that we would have eaten most anything, we ran across a deserted warehouse full of turnips and cabbages. We ate boiled cabbages and turnips until we couldn't hold anymore, and sticking a few of them in our packs started out again. At one place we found another warehouse filled with hundreds of cases of synthetic honey. We even ran across an old shed that had numbers of cases of matches stored in it. All this country that we were traversing had been fought over the last two or three weeks, and these were warehouses that had been abandoned by the German army. For about ten days we traveled in this manner, sometimes eating and sometimes not. As we drew closer to the lines we came upon a huge concentration camp filled with Russians. Russia had made a separate peace with Germany and its soldiers were immediately interned by the French. They were only half fed, and were a tough looking crowd. Chester and I presented ourselves to the Commander of the camp and told him we were on our way back to the lines and asked him for food and a chance to bath. He was kind enough to give to us a real meal in his officers quarters, let us take a hot bath, gave us some tobacco, and directed us to a truck company that was leaving for the front occupied by the 32nd division.

We hiked over to the truck company and discovered that the Captain in charge was Captain Riegel, formerly of the old Third Wisconsin and he had us get into a truck with him. We rode for possibly seven or eight hours, and the morning of November 11th we reached the lines and made our way back to Company "E" who at that time was in position near the city of Sedan and was preparing for another drive. We had a hard time getting up there on account of the ever present artillery firing but got safely through and met the old gang. It was about 10:45 A.M. when we finally got set and back into our old jobs. My old platoon had not replaced my job and I stepped right back into my position at company headquarters again. The Boche were laying down machine gun barrage on the positions, and although we lost several men wounded, we did not suffer any killed on that memorable day.

THE WAR'S OVER

By now we all suspicioned that something was in the air; although nothing was said our officers told us to lay low and wait for unexpected developments. The German army was on the run, and we did not think they would counter-attack, but we hardly expected to hear anything else. But it came—and at eleven o'clock sharp the order came to cease firing, that the war was over and the Allies had won. There were a few spasmodic shots, but in a few seconds all was quiet. For a few minutes there was a peculiar quiet, and then, without any ceremony, we crawled out of our concealment and built some fires. It was cold and frosty and a fire felt good, in fact it felt extra good to-day because we could make all the smoke we wanted to because t it would not be the signal for a barrage any more. The German Army, opposite, wasted no time in evacuating their positions, and running up white flags, they commenced the great withdrawal. And thus the war ended—a story written in blood, and suffering, and sacrifice, and perhaps sometimes needless slaughter.

The 32nd Division had been chosen as one of the American units to be a part of the Army of Occupation in Germany and preparations were begun at once for the long march into the Rhineland, a hike of several hundred miles. Some of the men were poorly equipped insofar as shoes were concerned, but no time was to be wasted and November 17th, 1918, we started our peacetime pursuit of our erstwhile enemy.

The march into Germany is in itself a story that would fill a book, and I will mention only the high lights of that famous march.

In November the weather, of course, is cold and frosty, although not so cold as in Wisconsin. We marched through the little Duchy of Luxemburg [sic] a beautiful little fairy land of ancient homes and castles and gardens. The countryside was simply beautiful at this time of the year and we enjoyed the scenery immensely. The marching, however, was terribly hard on account of the hard and stony roads, and since some of the men had poor shoes there was considerable suffering on the part of some of the fellows. As a rule we commenced the day's march about three o'clock in the morning and on some days marched until eleven at night. Some days we were just on the march four or five hours depending on how long it would take the German army to clear certain cities.

We were held in the city of Wasserbilling, Luxemburg [sic], for about three days waiting for the Germans to clear out, and this gave us a little chance to get our feet in shape and likewise recondition our equipment in general. We spent Thanksgiving day in this city and had a wonderful dinner of cold canned tomatoes, blood sausage, black coffee and bread. But we didn't care, the war was over and we had won, and nothing mattered anymore.

On December 1st, 1918, we crossed into Germany to the tune of "Yankee Doodle" and we all sang and whistled and had a great time. The German civilians stood in crowds and watched us quietly, it must have made them feel pretty bad alright. I understand that our outfit was the first American unit to step on German soil.

The hike through Luxemburg [sic] had been accomplished rather easily because the weather was near perfect. Now, however, it started to rain and the walking was a real hard task for everyone. Our packs weighed around forty pounds dry, and with the continuous rain I am sure five or six pounds were added. In addition to that our clothes soaked through and the constant rubbing of our service belts so chafed our hips that our clothes rubbed clear in the flesh. After the first couple of weeks, however, we camped in larger cities, and instead of sleeping in the open we were assigned to billets in German homes. This new method of camping brought out some interesting conditions, and gave us a good idea of German hospitality.

In some of the homes in which we were quartered the people were hostile and bitter, but the majority of the people were kindly towards us and treated us with the utmost consideration. They realized that we were simply under orders and that after all we were humans the same as they. It did not take them long to find out that we wouldn't harm anyone and if we wanted something we would pay for it. Some housewives even made hot soup for us and would serve it to us in their dining rooms. The German people were much more congenial than the French, whose country we had helped to save.

The illustration below is a picture of the bridge over which we crossed into Germany

Wasserbillig   Grenze Luxemburg-Deutschland

For a week or so, during the latter part of the march I was acting company commander, and at another time I was acting first sergeant. The company had been hard hit by an epidemic of flu and dysentery, and although I had a touch of the flu myself I was able to be on the job every day. This kept me busy night and day but I got a big kick out of it.

We crossed the Rhine river December 13th amid much shouting and singing and band playing, and we reached the town of Selters (Westerwald province) December 17th. We pulled into Selters around mid-night and as the houses we were to be billeted in were all marked with a white cross it was not such a hard job finding our places. It was cold and raining and we were covered with mud, and I do not imagine the German house wives enjoyed our tramping over their clean floors. We were glad to have the town of Selters assigned to us because it was a beautiful little place set deep in the hills and located on two railroads and near a river. It also had all modern city conveniences such as water, light, and so on.

Oscar Olson and I were assigned to the house owned by some people by the name of Merten; the household consisted of the mother, (about 74 years old) her daughter (about 35 years old), her son (a war veteran about 40 years old) and an adopted orphan about six years old. It was a fine family and we could see that we were going to get along fine here. They were refined, educated people, and owned a dray line and a fine piece of property. During our entire stay they were exceedingly kindly towards us, and we felt that we were a part of their family and treated them accordingly. Several times we brought them coffee, and white bread, and good beef, and sugar. It had been four years since they had had any of these luxuries and it did us good to watch them prepare dishes that they had not had for so long. And so it continued, and every day found us glad to get "home" after the days work. At Christmas time we even helped them trim the tree, and Oscar and I bought them each a present and had a nice time.

Our entire stay in Selters was devoted to guard duty and drilling. The drilling was more to keep in condition than anything else, and every one worked with a zest. My job was in the nature of a police job; I had the unpleasant task of clearing out the wine rooms every night after eleven o'clock in my area. My platoon was quartered in the depot and as that spot seemed to be the assembling place for the town each night there were times when I had my hands full trying to get some [of] the boys to go home. All in all, however, things went smoothly, and our stay in Selters was pleasant and interesting. There were occasional visits to Coblenz and other places of interest, and every effort was made to give each man a chance to view the places of historical interest.

The illustration below gives a view of the depot where my platoon was quartered.

Luftkurort Selters (Westerwald) - Bahnhof

I neglected to state that shortly after our arrival in Selters I was promoted to the rank of platoon sergeant in command of eight squads, with a total personnel of 72 men.

The 18th of April, 1919, was a memorable day for us because on that day we received orders to prepare to leave for the United States. No amount of writing could describe the wild scenes that followed this piece of news, there was just one continuous party for a solid week. There were farewell parties given by the civilians and local authorities, and our own officers just winked and let everyone celebrate as much as they wanted to. Oscar Olson and I were given a little farewell dinner by the Merton family. The manner in which the people of Selters feted the regiment was a wonderful testimonial as to the manner in which we had treated them; some of the people said that they actually hated to see us leave because they did not know what kind of order would prevail after we had gone. As things turned out, we were replaced by units of the 2nd Infantry, a regular army outfit. The people of Selters might have hated to see us go, but we did not feel that way at all, all we wanted to do was get home and get there quick.

All preparations were completed very quickly, and by the end of that week we were all ready to leave. Once again we were given physical examinations, and after the usual checking process was over we prepared for transportation to the point where our truck train was lined up to take us to the city of Bingen where we were to entrain for the seaport town of Brest for embarkation that was to bring us back to the States again. We marched possibly five miles before we reached the point where our trucks were lined up, and after much singing and band playing we piled into our assigned places in the trucks. Just a few minutes before we started, Otto Mai called to me and said there was an old lady looking for me, so I jumped out of the truck to investigate. Who should be standing there but Mrs. Merton. That old lady (she was at least 75 years old) had hiked all the way from Selters to bring me lunch she had prepared for me to eat on the train during the ride to the port of Brest. She again shook hands with me, and after handing me the lunch she again said good-bye.

It touched all of the fellows and I certainly thought that her long hike out to see me was a beautiful gesture of friendship, and symbolic of the treatment that we had received during the last four months. The truck train started almost immediately, and waving a last farewell to my good friend, we started off.

The truck ride was a short one, and in less than an hour we were at Bingen-on-the-Rhine and ready to entrain in AMERICAN box cars. After having ridden in dinky French cars so many times this sight of American box cars made us feel that we were riding in class. We loaded in, about sixty men to a car, and in less than an hour were on our way to France again. This time we were pulled by an American freight engine and we made excellent time all the way. The country we went through was beautiful, and being in April, everything was in full bloom. We had meals on board, and once or twice we detrained for a little leg-stretching. I had charge of the prisoners car so my ride was not quite so restful as it might have been as I had some bad actors to keep company. One of them, a Clarence Price from California, had tried to shoot me while we were in Germany, so I never left the car for any reason without taking him with me so I could keep an eye on him. But he behaved real well, possibly because I still carried my automatic, and nothing happened. In three days we reached Brest and were marched out to a camp on the outskirts of the town.

No time was wasted here, everything went at top speed, and aside from still another physical examination, we did nothing but wait for the time to embark. Our clothes were steamed out and sterilized and then we were ready to go.

On May 16th, 1919, we were all assembled, given a short talk by some high ranking officer (with nobody listening to him) and started the march to the pier. I have heard some cheering in my life but I never expect to hear such a yell as went up from 7500 of us when we sighted the transport George Washington lying in the harbor waiting to take us home. It was a real surprise, and everyone was absolutely satisfied. The loading process took only about a day, and without anymore ceremony than a blast from her whistle the transport started to move out toward the open sea. We all took a last look at France, (one can imagine what our feelings were), and then settled down for the return trip.

The ride across the Atlantic was uneventful. There were a couple od [sic] days of heavy fog, but otherwise the weather was great. We made wonderful time over a smooth sea, and on the sixth day we sighted the good old U.S.A. A person would think that there would be endless and wild cheering, but hardly a sound was made, we just stood and looked, thinking it was almost to good to be true. An hour or so after sighting land we came to the Statue of Liberty; the band played the National Anthem and we all stood on deck with our hats off. Shortly afterwards we passed the liner Martha Washington heading out to sea loaded with troops for the Army of Occupation; we gave them a good loud cheer and then headed for our bunks to roll our packs and get ready to disembark.

It was May 13th when we landed at Hoboken. We hiked immediately to a train that was waiting to transport us to Camp Merritt. Within six hours after leaving Hoboken we were at Merritt preparing for another examination. And another steaming of our clothing, preparatory for leaving for Camp Grant, Illinois, for final discharge. At this time Clarence Cleasby and I had to do part of the office work because our regular company clerk had been discharged immediately because of his residence in the East. The day after our arrival at Camp Merritt we again loaded onto trains and headed for Camp Grant and home.

We arrived at Camp Grant in the afternoon of May 16th, 1919, and immediately after arriving we all turned in whatever government property we still had and were given clearance papers. We were allowed to keep our uniforms, overcoats, helmets, shoes, shirts, and so on. All we had to turn in was actual firearms and mess supplies. Our gas masks were given to us for a present from Uncle Sam.

The next morning we were given our discharge papers, and believe it or not, were given another physical examination This was the final examination and it took nearly all day to complete it because entries had to be made on our service record. At the time of discharge I weighed 168 pounds, and was in pretty good condition.

It was an exciting period, and time went slowly for us. In the late afternoon we were paid off, and after another talk from our colonel, and a greeting from Captain Sortomme, we were put on troop trains for transportation to home stations.

The train ride to Eau Claire was one of the wildest ten hours that I ever expect to see, how the train managed to stay on the track was a mystery to me. But we made it, and everyone was in presentable condition, both internally and externally, when we finally did reach home early in the morning of May 17th, 1919.

We pulled into the Northwestern Depot, and this time I am sure the whole town was on hand, and what a welcome it was. Those who had seemed comparatively small children were now young men and women, and those who had seemed cheerful and happy at other homecomings were now bent and broken. But all in all it was a great crowd, and with all the fellows trying to find their families and sweethearts there certainly was plenty of confusion and noise. I found my family after a few minutes and there was a happy re-union. Kenneth had grown so big, but Ella, Minnie, Olga, Albert, and the rest looked just the same with the exception of father who had become aged and stooped. We had a lively time for a few minutes and then left for home; home that had almost seemed like a dream a short time ago; home that we thought we would never see again; home that we vowed we would never leave again; home that we had called for when we lay wounded and gasping on the battle-field just five months ago; home—the grandest and most beautiful haven on earth.

When I reached the house there on the front porch my folks had hung a big flag. I stopped for a moment of – I don't know what I did stop for, just to look I suppose – and then we all went in together. Even my old dog, Spitz, gave me a rousing welcome. I walked through all the rooms, it seemed so long ago since I was last here. This is the place where all men belong, this is the place we all fought to uphold, this is the name of the place that will keep us out of another war, HOME, and brothers, and sisters, and wives, and children, and memories.

- - - - - - - - - -

THE END

✠

The following countries participated in the World War.

The Allies - sometimes referred to as the Holy Alliance:

Montenegro	The United States	Russia
Greece	France	England
Belgium	Italy	Brazil
Portugal	Serbia	Roumania
Japan	China	

John B. Smith

The enemy - although popularly referred to as Germany - consisted of the following:

Germany   Turkey   Austria

Hungary   Bulgaria

The various colonies of the above nations also participated in the war by furnishing man power, supplies, high taxation on Allied goods, and in other ways. The above powers, however, are the ones between whom war was declared and wages.

✠

During the period from March 1917 to May 1919 Company "E" was represented by troops from 40 different states and 5 foreign countries. This was due to replacements because of deaths and injuries.

The various states were represented as follows:

Alabama	3	Nebraska	11
Arkansas	18	New Hampshire	1
California	29	New Jersey	1
Colorado	1	New York	7
Connecticut	1	North Dakota	1
District [of] Columbia	3	Ohio	12
Florida	2	Oklahoma	5
Georgia	1	Oregon	22
Idaho	3	Pennsylvania	7

Illinois	40	South Carolina	1
Indiana	11	South Dakota	3
Iowa	7	Utah	1
Kansas	4	Tennessee	7
Kentucky	23	Texas	11
Louisiana	10	Virginia	2
Massachusetts	2	Washington	18
Michigan	6	West Virginia	3
Minnesota	25	Wisconsin	255
Missouri	10	Wyoming	1
Montana	13		

Foreign Countries were represented as follows:

Canada	4	Greece	1
Ireland	2	Italy	2
Norway	1		

The total strength, therefore, of Company "E", including replacements that were listed on our roster was:

--- 595 Officers and Men

Original strength: ---250 Officers and Men

War casualties --- 345

REMEMBRANCES

There are various incidents that come to mind concerning my different sojourns with Company "E", and as I think of them I will write them down just as they come to me.

✠

Our travels along the Mexican Border probably was mixed with more humorous events than in 1917 because of the difference of the times.

I shall never forget the sleepy southern nights we put in at guard duty while in San Antonio, Texas. One night Clarence Cleasby and I were on the same guard detail, our post of duty being the quartermaster's tent. We would walk our post until we were so sleepy that we could hardly see, then to rouse ourselves we would run our post to keep awake. Clarence made the mistake one night of sitting down on a pile of empty bandoliers to catch his breath. No sooner had he sat down than he was sound asleep. When the time came for his relief I marched up with the rest of the guard detail; he sort of roused himself, but in the meantime both of his legs had gone to sleep and as he attempted to stand up he fell flat on his face and was unable to make his legs function for a couple of minutes. In the meantime the sergeant of the guard (I think it was Bill Christensen) was bawling him out and we were all laughing until we could hardly stand. Clarence never did hear the end of it. Another time we were again walking the same post, this time in pairs. The quartermaster owned a pet goat and we kept on teasing the thing to pass the time away. When the goat was irritated he would let out loud snorts like a person snoring, and of course we got a lot of fun out of it. But for that escapade we had to spend a night in the guard house for keeping half the battalion awake.

❖

In 1916, the call of taps was just so much music as far as getting in was concerned. After retreat we could go down town and stay as long as we liked, the only thing that mattered was being on time for morning roll call - reveille. We would get in all the way from midnight to five in the morning. One morning just after we had "fallen in" we saw a staggering figure trying to run up the company street. It turned out to be Henry Lien, our bugler, and he was plenty drunk. He was trying to make the street before the roll would be called. Just as he pulled up even with the first sergeants then the stumbled on a rope and fell on his face. As he lay there with a sick look on his face a snake about a foot long crawled out of his shirt (he had purchase it down town and forgotten about it). You should have heard him yell - he thought he was having D.T.'s and that he was "seeing snakes". The last time I saw him, six or seven years ago, he was still being kidded about it.

✠

The two most "pestered" men in the company were E.B. and L.M. As soldiers they were total failures. E. would never take a bath unless a couple of fellows grabbed him and made him do it. Once we gave him a shower with all his clothes on in an attempt to cure him, but without results. He just didn't like water although when all dressed up he looked fine.

L.M. was just simply "queer" and did not know what it was all about. We used to call him Saginaw (that is where tanglefoot fly-paper is made). He was assistant to the cook and a hard worker, but as a soldier he was a misfit. He was finally discharged and sent back to Eau Claire as disabled; he was given a medical discharge in order to keep his record clear because in his own way he was really a fine fellow.

✣

The latter part of October 1918, Captain Normington recommended me as the one enlisted man from Company I to attend the officers' school at Belfort. The war ended, of course, before the time I was to leave, which would have been December 1st, 1918. I at least had the satisfaction of knowing that I had been appointed, and an as only one man was chosen from each company I felt highly honored.

✣

One of the interesting things we learned at the Gas School at Gondrecourt was how to shovel gas with a canvas shovel. The instructors would lay down a gas attack (using real phosgene gas) and after it had settled into the system of trenches we would have to take our shovels and shovel it out where the breeze would scatter it and make the trench safe for occupancy. The gases used during the war were all heavier than air so that it would cling to the ground. [see page 86]

✣

German airplanes would frequently drop propaganda on our lines in which we would be told how "hopeless" our cause was, and that we might just as well lay down our arms and quit. It gave us a big laugh.

At one point, during the fighting, we captured a fair sized city that had been quite a railroad center. There were hundreds of Belgian locomotives on the tracks that the Germans had confiscated so that the Belgians would have no means of escape. There were also warehouses filled to the roof with church bells that evidently the Boche would use for casting guns etc. One warehouse was filled with French harvest machinery; another was loaded with cream separators.

✤

There was a scarcity of meat among the German soldiers, and we saw plenty of evidence of cases in which they had eaten their horses, and in one instance even a dog was eaten. In Germany I was present when a butcher bought one [of] our mules for his meat market to be sold as soup meat. The mule had stumbled and broken his leg and had to be shot.

✤

A great favorite with the people of Germany is rabbit meat. I have eaten it many times and thought that I was eating chicken. Nearly every home has its rabbit hutch in the back yard and is one of the principle sources of food, particularly in rural communities.

✤

For a considerable time after the conclusion of the

war there was considerable argument as to whether or not the 32ⁿᵈ Division engaged in any hand-to-hand fighting during its campaigns after leaving Alsace-Lorraine. The German raid on our Third Platoon at P.C. Stockette could be classed as hand-to-hand, although that fight consisted mostly of pitching hand grenades at close quarters and rifle and pistol fire at close range. In the darkness of the early morning, and due to the fact that the Germans took their wounded back with them after the raid, and die also to the fact that the one dead the Germans left was shot and stabbed several times it was hard to find evidence that would class the raid and its subsequent fighting as hand-to-hand.

At the Second Battle of the Marne, however, there was no question as to the fighting with knives with the German defenders in bright sunshine with plenty of unwilling witnesses to the sickening sight. Richard McGrath, our runner, stood less than two feet from me when I rammed my bayonet into the neck of a Boche soldier who was trying to kill our Captain Sortomme who was some five or six feet behind us. (It was this act that brought me my recommendation for a citation). Several of the other fellows likewise were doing some fast bayonet work trying to dislodge the machine gun nest in the strip of trees.

Some years later, when reading the memoirs of our Commanding General, William G. Hahn, I discovered that he had received reports of bayonet fighting but the report had come to him as a rumor rather than as an official report. As two of our officers were present at the fight (Captain Sortomme, and Lieut. John Martin) the fact that it was not properly reported accounts for General Hahn's statement in his memoirs (written shortly before his death in 1923). This fact may be verified by consulting his articles appearing in the Milwaukee Journal the summer of 1922, and copies of which are in my possession at this time.

It would seem, therefore, that my platoon engaged in the only actual bayonet fight accredited to the 32nd Division, even though it was not officially recorded.

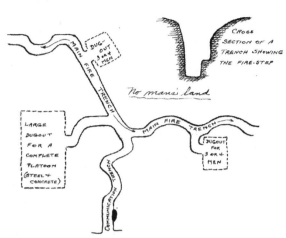

The above sketch is the general layout of "P.C. STOCKETTE" in Alsace. Trenches were about 5 to 6 feet deep and 3 to 5 feet wide at the top. The small dugouts were about 6 feet below trench level and the large one about ten feet below trench level. This layout was perhaps a half-mile long overall.

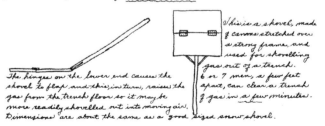

This is a shovel, made of canvas stretched over a strong frame, and used for shovelling gas out of a trench. 6 or 7 men, a few feet apart, can clear a trench of gas in a few minutes.

The hinge on the lower end causes the shovel to flap and this, in turn, raises the gas from the trench floor so it may be more readily shovelled out into moving air. Dimensions are about the same as a good sized snow shovel.

A gas shell, of the type used in the later stages of the war, was built along these general lines. The liquid, which evaporated and formed gas when exposed to the air, was contained in a glass vial or, tube, within the shell itself.

- FIRING PIN.
- CAP MECHANISM.
- GUN POWDER (NOT T.N.T.)
- GLASS TUBE OF LIQUID GAS.

Gas shells explode with a sort of dull, ripping, report. They do not explode with the crashing explosion of a high-explosive shell.

Commonly used hand grenades are sketched below.

 FRENCH   U.S.    GERMAN

This type, above, about the size of a tennis ball was set-off by striking the pin against the helmet. It explodes in 10 seconds. (Also made in incendiary form for burning etc)

The "mills" grenade used by U.S. Army broke into small pieces when exploded and was less dangerous to handle than the type on the left. (10 second type)

The "potato" masher was set off by jerking out the string protruding from the handle. The weight was about the same as the american grenade and was easily handled.

The U.S. Army rifle-grenades (V.B.) were powerful instruments and required skill in handling. On the left, below, is a diagram of the rifle attachment, and on the right is the grenade itself:

The funnel-like attachment fits over the muzzle of the rifle and the grenade inside. The rifle bullet carries the grenade with it. In firing, the butt of the rifle is held on the ground and the range of the grenade depends on the angle on which the rifle is held.

The grenade is about 2 inches in diameter and 3 inches long. It was developed during the world war.

HERBERT HOOVER

August 28, 1936

Dear Mr. Smith:

I shall be glad to have you have a letter from me to be added to the many which you will no doubt collect for your book of experiences.

The period of the war was indeed a great period in the world's history. It summoned the best of courage and devotion and self-sacrifice in our people. But the results of the Great War, like the results of any war, are a long-continued series of grave liabilities to mankind.

Yours faithfully,

Herbert Hoover

Mr. J. B. Smith
3423 North 15th Street
Milwaukee, Wisconsin

623 MIRADA
STANFORD UNIVERSITY
CALIFORNIA

I only saw General Pershing three times, once in Alsace, once near Chateau Thierry and once when he reviewed us in Germany. His personality was so outstanding that one could almost feel he was the commander without being told.

JOHN J. PERSHING
WASHINGTON

May 28, 1936.

Sgt. John B. Smith,
3423 North 15th St.,
Milwaukee, Wisconsin.

My dear Sgt. Smith:

I have read with much interest your letter of May 26th describing the story you have written of your experiences with the fine old 32nd Division of the A.E.F. It should be a splendid souvenir of your service to pass on to posterity.

With best wishes, believe me

Sincerely yours,

John J. Pershing

"CALL TO QUARTERS"

As I sit here, nearly twenty years after those three tragic years, in a warm comfortable room, with my wife and daughter nearby, there wells up within me a choking, bursting feeling.

There never passes a day but that I think of the eighty-thousand fellow Americans who lie buried in the great cemeteries of France. But for the simple expedient of laying down a pen the majority of those men might still be living with us.

There rarely passes a day but that I think of the unknown soldiers buried overseas – no mark to tell who they are – but who sleep in eternal glory, known only to God.

I also honor the thousands who are confined in

hospitals and institutions, with twisted bodies and minds, and eyes that stare vacantly towards Heaven, wondering who cares and whether or not their sacrifices were really worth while.

✠

I know some little boys who are just now of the age where games of war, and guns, occupy their play-time. I often wish that there might be some way in which the sale of such toys and games might be made punishable. The time will come soon enough, as it has for all generations, when they too will have to march away from homes and a family, and friends, and perhaps be the victims of another great war to end war.

I know, too, a little girl who loves to play at being nurse. May it be her exceptional good fortune that her nursing will be confined to some peace-time incidents rather than the wholesale butcheries of an unreasoning war.

✠

I have tried to set forth in the preceding pages, my life during the years 1916, 1917, 1918, 1919, There are many things that cannot be written – things that a soldier can only think about – certain feelings and emotions that will not fit into words. It is my sincere hope that perhaps someone may profit by my experience, and also perhaps help him, or her, to be a better and more understanding American.

MEMORIAL DAY 1970

Today we have met together to honor our heroic dead. A thousand battles of land, and sea, and air, echo the glory of their deeds. Under the quiet sod, or beneath the murmuring waves, wherever they may rest, <u>this</u> is a day of remembrance. In the destinies of men, their souls go marching on. Because of them our lives are free; because of them our nation lives. They fought for us; and they fell. Now, with one accord, in deepest reverence, we do honor them.

It is now over 100 years since General Logan issued the proclamation that May 30th should hereafter be set aside, each year, to honor the memory of those brave men and women who served their country in its times of need, and who now rest in eternal peace and glory, and lie sleeping in hallowed and sacred ground.

Little did he realize then, that thousands more would die in the defense of this nation, in 8 or 9 major conflicts that have followed the Civil War, and average of perhaps one in every 20 years. Little did he realize, then, that uncounted thousands more would lie sick, and helpless, in veterans' hospitals, and elsewhere, paying their share of the cost of this priceless heritage we call liberty, many of whom are patiently awaiting the final roll-call when Taps shall sound, and they will be tenderly wrapped within the folds of the flag they loved. Yes – the price of liberty and freedom is great indeed.

Sometimes some people wonder if the cost is worth it. It is a sad, but heart-rending fact, that great nations, in this supposedly enlightened age, must, like some immature people, resort to fighting and killing to resolve their differences. But, it seems, that is the way it is ordained; and so it has been ever since history has been recorded. The scriptures say: "Come, let us reason together." But it appears that certain of those who rule and govern, ignore this sacred admonition.

Indeed, the cost of being a free people has been paid in part by the blood and sacrifices of our forefathers, and is still being paid for on today's battlefields, by the sacrifices of some of your own children, and by the anguish and anxieties of you mothers and fathers.

On the other hand, these brave men and women, whose memory we honor on this Memorial Day, gladly offered their lives, in order that you and I, and future generations, might be free men, and that this dear America of ours might take its rightful place in the family of nations, and be a symbol of everything that stands for the God-given rights of all people, regardless of race, color, or creed. <u>Americans are like that.</u>

Oh, there are many of our citizens who violently criticize, and revile, our government. There are many who categorically oppose our country's involvement in foreign affairs; they march, and demonstrate, and protest, and carry signs that often times are insulting to those of us who love our country. And there are many who feel that our military operations overseas are resulting in needless loss of life. Others maintain that America has "lost face", as it were, because of these things. Others feel that we have made monumental blunders in our present war efforts. But, it is the <u>prerogative</u> of an American to criticize and find fault; moreover, it is the right of all citizens in a free land, such as ours. Our constitution grants that right. But thanks be to God, in spite of all criticism, a small part of which may be justifiable, - but much of which is entirely unforgivable, - we are still firmly and solidly united as a nation; passionately proud of our heritage, and loyal to our government, and proud of our country's efforts in the endless fight to make all men free and equal.

We are inordinately proud of the fact that we help to feed the hungry and the helpless of all lands, regardless of their political alliances. Let us all be glad, and eternally thankful, that in these days of our great abundance, our charity extends beyond the seas, and that we are proud to share a reasonable portion of our surplus with people – especially little children – who have never known the comforts, or enjoyed the plenty, such as we sometimes are apt to take for granted.

Let us here remember, and be proud of the words of our martyred, and immortal President, Abraham Lincoln, who said: "With malice toward none, and with charity for all." Certainly those words are part of an American's creed. God grant us the wisdom and the courage to keep it that way.

Let us be forever glad, and eternally grateful, that we live in a country where there is no "iron curtain"; where there is not "wall of infamy"; where people may worship when, and where they please; where our children are still a part of their families; where there is still free enterprise, and free elections to choose our form of government; and a multitude of other great freedoms, too numerous to count, with which you and I have been blest. But let us not be complacent, and take America for granted. All that we have today, has been bought and paid for, by those unselfish comrades whose memory we honor on this Memorial Day.

When we reflect on all of the things our country has done for us, and all of the privileges we enjoy, it is inconceivable that anyone would spend their energy in trying to undermine the foundations of this bulwark of freedom and democracy that has stood the test of time.

These are but a few of the things for which our comrades of all wars and conflicts fought and died. These are some of the things we would especially remember on this Memorial Day, and all of the days that will follow.

This is why, today, we lovingly and tenderly strew flowers on their graves and on each of them place a little American flag, or a wreath, or perhaps a white cross, in testimony of our love and remembrance of them.

This is why, today, we fire a salute in their honor. This is why today the bugler sounds Taps. This is why, today, our buddies and comrades, and our children, carrying the Stars and Stripes, proudly march through our cities to sacred and consecrated places such as this.

This is why the bands of our schools play martial music. This is why we stand with uncovered heads with our right hand over our heart, as we listen to the stains of our beloved National Anthem. This is why, you and I today have renewed allegiance to our country and have re-dedicated ourselves to its service.

And at the close of this observance in memory of

those who gave their last full measure of devotion, let us gratefully lift our hearts toward Heaven, and give thanks to our Creator, for the privilege of <u>being an American</u>.

And today, if the Red of the Stars and Stripes seems more crimson, and if the White appears a little whiter, and if the Blue appears to be deeper, and if the Stars in their field of blue seem to be brighter than they were yesterday, it is because you, and I, have counted the cost, and have not forgotten those who rest in eternal peace and glory, and have re-dedicated ourselves to the service, and the everlasting glory, of the United States of America.

Lake Mills
Memorial Day
May 30, 1970
J.B. Smith (Jack)

41850071R00063

Made in the USA
Lexington, KY
29 May 2015